Praise for *A Million-Dollar Bill*

Eric Paul Shaffer's poems are always filled with clear light and fresh air. They restore deep attention and gratitude, a rebalancing between land and sky.

—Naomi Shihab Nye, Chancellor of the Academy of American Poets, 2009-2015, and author of *Fuel* and *Transfer*

The poems in A Million-Dollar Bill represent Shaffer's thoughtful presence in the world at his (and our) big-hearted best. His poems are full stories in small frames, always sharply said, never sentimental, relentlessly true, sensuously rich, always welcoming us in.

—J.D. Whitney, author of *Grandmother Says, All My Relations*, and *Sweeping the Broom Shorter*

A Million-Dollar Bill is Eric Paul Shaffer's most imaginative book yet! With unparalleled accuracy and clarity, Shaffer's astute observations turn the world on its ear through your ear. Read these poems aloud and often.

—Sara Backer, author of *American Fuji* and *Bicycle Lotus*

Eric Paul Shaffer's poems must be radically après-garde because I swear I sometimes understand every word. It's as if Shaffer's appointed himself defender of those corniest of literary values: clarity and precision. He writes with a naive sense of wonder and play, as if earnest communication were still possible between human beings. You'd almost have to think the man enjoys being alive.

—M. Thomas Gammarino, author of *King of the Worlds, Big in Japan*, and *Jellyfish Dreams*

A Million-Dollar Bill reached me just in time. After going without any new Shaffer poems for eleven years, I was beginning to wonder if I was going to die of thirst, reading my way across the Great American Poetry Desert. I'm okay now. Thirst quenched but hoping I don't have to wait that long again.

—Red Pine (Bill Porter), translator of *The Collected Songs of Cold Mountain* and author of *Zen Baggage: A Pilgrimage to China*

A Million-Dollar Bill

Other Books by Eric Paul Shaffer

Poetry

Kindling: Poems from Two Poets (Longhand Press; with James Taylor III)

RattleSnake Rider (Longhand Press)

Portable Planet (Leaping Dog Press)

Living at the Monastery, Working in the Kitchen (Leaping Dog Press)

Lāhaina Noon: Nā Mele O Maui (Leaping Dog Press)

Road Sign Suite: Across America and Again (Obscure Publications)

Restoring ~~Lady~~ Liberty (Obscure Publications)

Even Further West (Unsolicited Press)

Green Leaves: Selected & New Poems (Coyote Arts)

Fiction

You Are Here (Obscure Publications)

The Felony Stick (Leaping Dog Press)

Burn & Learn, or Memoirs of the Cenozoic Era (Leaping Dog Press)

Criticism

How I Read Gertrude Stein by Lew Welch (Grey Fox Press)

A Million-Dollar Bill

Poems

Eric Paul Shaffer

Albuquerque, New Mexico | 2024

A Million-Dollar Bill.
Copyright © 2016, 2024 Eric Paul Shaffer
Originally published by Grayson Books, West Hartford, Connecticut, 2016.
Second edition published by Coyote Arts, Albuquerque, New Mexico, 2024.

Interior & Cover Design by Cindy Stewart
Author Photo by Melanie Van der Tuin

SECOND EDITION

All rights reserved. No part of this publication may be reproduced, stored in a retrieval system or transmitted in any form or by any means, electronic, mechanical, photocopying, recording or otherwise without the prior permission of the publisher.

ISBN   978-1-58775-044-1 (paper)
           978-1-58775-045-8 (e-book)
Library of Congress Control Number: 2023944638

Coyote Arts LLC
PO Box 6690
Albuquerque, New Mexico 87197-6690 USA
coyote-arts.com

2 4 6 8 9 7 5 3 1

Contents

Watermelon Seeds

Watermelon Seeds	13
A Telephone	14
The Printer	15
An Alchemy of Soap and Seeds and Cinders	16
The Woman I Might Have Been	18
Exploring the House Next Door When Nobody's Home	20
Cleaning Up After the Storm	21
A Festival of Crescents	22
Fortuitous	23
The Famous Poet's Wife	25
How I Lost My Library Card	26
The Evil Eric	27
For the Anniversary of My Death	29
For All You Touch	30
River Eye	31

A Silver Flask

Illumination	35
Among the Roots	36
McNeil, Arkansas, 1942	37
City of the Anti-Ghosts	38
Monopoly	40
The Kansas City Grand Emporium Blues	41
Should Have Seen It Coming	42
A Silver Flask	43
The Priest at Galileo's Deathbed	44
Midnight, Snow and Stars	47
Planets, Houses, and the Night Always Above Us	48
On the Occasion of Andy's Cancer Diagnosis	49
How to Successfully Flee the Storm	51
Hart Crane's Borrowed Raincoat	52
Man Overboard	53
An Anatomy of the Celestial	55

The Glad Reaper

Matching Coffee Mugs	59
The Woman Who Clears the Way	60
Blessings	61
The Awk Word	62
Eating Crow	63
The Word-Swallower	64
The Lessons of Moonlight	66
The Glad Reaper	67
The Whistle	68
The Godzilla Delusion	69
My Brother's Keeper	71
The Eye of Winter	73
Our Little Piece of Sky	74
Luminaria on Wellesley Drive: Albuquerque, 1978	75
A Million-Dollar Bill	76
Notes	79
Acknowledgments	80
About the Author	82

Watermelon Seeds

Watermelon Seeds

    Setting the first icy slice on my paper plate, my mother warned me
not to swallow watermelon seeds. A vine would sprout from my navel.

    For the rest of my life, all would ask only about the fruit sprung
from beneath my shirt, waiting for my curved, slender sentences as long
        as the flourishing vine. All I know is this. A tough cord

    of broad leaves burst from my belly. Flowers folded into fruit
and swelled with wet, pink flesh, sugar, and light, every one a world

        within a smooth, striped rind in a green as deep as summer.
Each slick, black seed between sticky fingers was as ripe with promise
    as a period, all those flat, black dots, an ever-lengthening ellipsis

leading to a day I might speak of the mystery erupting from my guts.
        All summer, I swallowed every seed.

A Telephone

I hum in your hand, a tune familiar as childhood chants
with rhymes forgotten. My voice is not the one you wish
to hear. What I can tell you is only what anyone knows.

I am the river of the tremendous and the trivial swollen
with stolen debris, a torrent become a trickle littering
the shocked and sodden land as the startled moon stares

from muddy, root-framed pools. The tragedies I tell are
timeless and new, new, new, new, new as the daily blab,

live, local, and late-breaking, with details petty, pointless,
and accurate as an arc of pain. I'm a dark, unplumbed ear,
faceless, with countless tongues recounting endless tales.

I am blameless and empty as a shell slicing a sole strolling
pathless, printed sand, seeking treasure on the tide at dawn.

In repose, I'm a dull monument to silence sunk in shades
concealing nothing. I am the messenger of a thousand

wings and acts and scenes, unscathed in the denouement,
no question remaining, no revelation unmade. Mine is
not my own, yet I carry voices from arrogant origins

through the sky, sun, and stars to ends I cannot imagine
till I speak. I repeat nothing. I translate every syllable

into an exact language cupped in the claws of sparrows
and squirrels, blazing under sun and clouds, whispering
through trees and ice and hands and wind. My words

leave the fingerprint of speech on the ideal. My ring
is eternal. My power is in the line, electric and current.

The Printer

My last command to "Print" secreted a page crowned
with a green streak in the shape of a heart but nothing
        in black and white. The inkless page was a puzzle.

When I unfurled gray plastic doors and removed the trays
of empty sheets, there was a miracle within. That recent spill

        of coffee laid down the grounds for something green.
I drew the cartridge out, and through the hole, I stared
into a new world. Sprouts of that vibrant shade we know

so well from the forest trail and the newly-grooved garden
shone within. Those first pouting pairs of rounded leaves,
            like hands cupped to receive the sky,

        rose between metal tracks and plastic walls, gleaming
with the light I let in. I had no choice. I turned the machine

        into a planter and brought the soil seedlings crave.
Now, I write each word by hand, all my letters loopy
        and cursive, and soon, I'll be harvesting beans.

An Alchemy of Soap and Seeds and Cinders

In the glass gallon jug discarded in the weedy ditch
was an inch of sudsy pink, and I knew I'd found

the makings of magic. Lifted with the ring at the lip,
the muddy glass was crystal, and the soap a potion
with a tint of promise. The sky was gray, the street

was gray, and I yearned to do something spectacular.
Magic is long days of play without consequences,

and, too young to spell a word of more than seven
letters, I believed. Through the narrow neck of glass,
I sprinkled crushed cinders from a church parking lot

and quartz pebbles flecked with mica I knew was gold.
I stuffed down stems of grass, leaves of maples, a rose

petal from Mrs. Perkle's garden, and, the crowning touch,
three winged white seeds from dandelions in the ditch.
I swirled the mixture in the jar, spoke magic words,

and pronounced the transformation complete. Not one
of my friends believed magic could come from me,

and none would drink. I taunted them for cowardice
and raised the jug to my lips. I drank. I drank deeply,
but managed only a few swallows before my throat

began to burn. I choked and coughed, spitting pink.
My legs wobbled, my eyes dimmed, and as I swayed,

the jug fell from limp fingers and spun in the cinders,
spraying the rest of my magic in a sudden soapy arc.
The fire on my tongue announced I'd made more

than magic, and I ran for home, past red-brick duplexes
and brown lawns stricken with poverty and poor soil,

and as I sprinted down the street, bubbles flowed
from my mouth with every breath, iridescent spheres
floating in a line behind me as I ran to our dark door.

In that moment, magic marked my way, every stinging
step on that root-buckled sidewalk, a gleam in a gray day,

an alchemy of soap and seeds and cinders. As I bolted
to the door, bubbles rose from my mouth, each a new
world of roiling rainbows, a word bursting to be heard.

The Woman I Might Have Been

Regina was the name chosen for the woman I might have been,
                had I been born a girl. I imagine her schoolmates
tormenting her on the playground, rhyming her name

with the coveted cleft in the fork of the female, but she
                would have forgiven them. The woman I might have been
would have loved her surly brother and kept him from the trouble

he constantly sought, in a way I never could. The woman
                I might have been would have been a beloved older sister
who taught her two younger sisters about knitting, algebra,

the Beatles, and preparing for proms with boys
                they carefully picked out together. The woman
I might have been would have been the first-chair flute

in the all-state school orchestra. The woman I might have been
                would have been a perfect daughter, leaving college
to come home when her father emptied the bank accounts

and abandoned the family. The woman I might have been
                would have signed her mother into the mental ward,
as I did, but she would have visited every day, played pinochle

with her mother and the other inmates, smuggling them all
                the magazines, candy, and cigarettes they craved.
The woman I might have been would have been happy

to bring her mother home, nurse her gently back into the world,
                and cry with her as quietly as widowed sisters.
She would have taken a job to meet the mortgage payment

and paid the grocery bills and handled car repairs.
                The woman I might have been would have made
everyone proud by marrying a man on the brink of wealth,

having the right number of exceptional children, and placing them
                                    in private schools and ivy league universities
on the respectable, elder coast of America. The woman

I might have been would have vacationed in Barbados,
          saved her baby sister from the man who was beating her,
given sound financial advice to her eternally lackluck brother,

and stood applauding longest at the Broadway premiere
                   of her middle sister blooming brilliantly into a star.
She would have had a long, happy life with a silver, a gold,

even a diamond anniversary with a man who loved her deeply,
             surrounded by all of her lovely children, grandchildren,
and her great-grandchildren, especially the youngest girl

who called her Reggie, as the whole family laughed. The woman
                  I might have been, the woman no one will ever know,
but for me, would even have forgiven me for taking her place

in my life, forgiving me in a way I could never have forgiven her.

Exploring the House Next Door
When Nobody's Home

The basement door unlocked, we entered, alert to every fan and floorboard.
          The fierce blue eye of the furnace was our only light, and she flicked
                    on fluorescent tubes. Shadows scattered behind washer and dryer,
fled into shelves of stacked boxes of games like *Candyland* and *Life* and *Sorry*.

          Many times, we'd played here, but with no friends to lead us, the rooms
were vaulted chambers in a castle abandoned to the wicked. Glazed shafts
                    of bamboo on the bar gleamed, and bottles brimmed with amber,
          gold, and silver. We opened them all, and sipped from some, grinning,

tasting fire from cut-glass tumblers. Our hands entwined, we slowly climbed
          the risers to the living room. The TV stared, and we saw ourselves
          taller but smaller, in its glassy eye. The rooms were larger with only us
                    to fill them. We slid from kitchen to dining room to hall.

          The bedroom was majestic, bed inviting and unmade, with afternoon light
framed in the intimate folds of heavy curtains, inexplicably rich and dark.
                    Outside, a car started, and our friends were calling, but within,
          we gazed on a new mystery. Together on the bed, warm from the sun,

     delicious to the skin, she turned to me. In that light, we saw each other only
               once. Her arms encircled me, and I embraced her. We began.
                         Those strange and intimate rooms blazed and roared around us.
The house did not belong to us, and what we stole there would never be ours.

Cleaning Up After the Storm

From the beach this morning, the sound of waves breaking on the reef
is lost in wind rushing through palm leaves. Beneath cloudless blue,

a solid line of litter marks the sand, sticks and bark and leaves and trash
       left by high tide after last night's deluge washed the cliffs clean,
and to the horizon, the sea is brown with earth. The storm was Biblical,

       battering the island with crashes and flashes. Rain tore laundry
from lines and floated rubber slippers to the beach. Nobody could sleep

through the lightning, and thunder rattled the panes in their casings.
Dogs quivered beneath the bed. Wind banged doors in their frames
so loud I didn't hear the neighbor knocking, but the candles kept us

      awake, and I finally saw him dripping on the porch. Today,
he went home to inspect his house. His car is sunk to the door panels,

his living room floor lost beneath muddy water, and his garden is gone.
Newly-painted kitchen walls are streaked with leaks he never knew
before. His power is out. From puddles, I pluck floating clothespins

and search for gardening gloves, beach mats, and dog food bowls.
He smiles as he splashes to the wall of lava rock between our yards,

pointing at the steep cliff behind me, rising hundreds of feet skyward
from papaya trees, coconut palms, heliconia, red ginger, and mango.

I turn, and he says, "Look at that. Look how green the mountain is."

A Festival of Crescents
one for Andy

On the day of the eclipse, he was well on his way when the sky darkened.
The first shadow was like a cloud across the sun, but the darkness grew.
He would never reach home in time to cast the dwindling image on a sheet

of paper, not with pin and glass still on the kitchen table. Darkness swelled.
The birds grew quiet. A chill breeze carried the wail of a distant siren, eerie

in noon twilight. Newscasters warned never to stare at the sun. Even a peek

at the shadow devouring light might blind, but he wanted to see darkness
make a moon of the sun. He walked beneath an oak, staring at the sidewalk,

and there, a festival of crescents flickered at his feet. Thousands of glittering
images of the sun refracted through living leaves, and his was a path through
the shifting shape of light as darkness plunges through the heart and emerges.

Fortuitous

Shakespeare class was on the third floor. Wide were the windows,
but it was Indiana, and there was nothing to see. The plays revealed
the better view, so I read every assignment. I was lucky enough

to sit by Claire, the most beautiful girl in the class. Doctor Locke
lectured with a vengeance. Like God, he knew all, was determined
to tell us everything, and test us. I knew nothing, so I was enthralled.

Claire was lovely and distracted. During a lecture on *King Lear,*
she whispered, "I've always wanted to meet my father." Later,
we sat on the auditorium steps. She told me her father abandoned

the family when she was two years old, stole the cash, the car,
and her mother's cousin, then fled Texas. I was ecstatic. Guys
glared, thinking I had lucked out and Claire was my girlfriend.

After years of searching, she'd found her father. He would arrive
on a bus from Reno on Monday. She could hardly wait. I knew
Julius Caesar was due on Monday. Hugging me and laughing,

she said a social worker retiring next week spoke to her father
only last month. Her eye was sharp enough to recognize him
through twenty-two years, unshaven cheeks, and a torn, blurry

black-and-white photo Claire's mother wasn't even sure was him.
She laid a hand on my arm, and I couldn't breathe. She thought
she was lucky to finally find her father after decades of desertion.

Falstaff fled the threat of death for the same crime. She'd spoken
with her father on the phone. She was delighted, but I wondered
where he'd been: watching *Oprah* from jail in Tampa, sweeping

a bar in Costa Rica, squatting in subways in New York, sleeping
under a dumpster in a Toronto alleyway. What vermin, diseases,
conditions, and disorders had he gathered? She'd be more careful

feeding a stray dog and luckier to find one. I recalled the Thane
of Cawdor and the three witches, yet Claire never even considered
she might one day wish she'd never met her father and how easy

that would have been had she never looked. Had she learned nothing
from *Hamlet*? "Fortune favors the foolish," remarked Dr. Locke,
suited in silver, striding imperiously back and forth before our desks,

chain-smoking and pontificating. And he immediately digressed,
impressing me by noting many speakers of English misuse the word
fortuitous. Even educated people are often inaccurate and mistaken

about the meaning. "We mislead ourselves whenever we choose
the wrong word, and here's a fine instance. *Fortuitous* simply means
chance, though most think it means *good fortune.*" After her father

arrived, Claire quit school. None knew whether by chance or design.
I never saw her again, but my new repute led to Sandra, equally cute
and more eager for my affections. Years later, when I finally read

Strunk and White, I found Dr. Locke's fortuitous insight on page 48.
Luck, it seems, consists of what any one of us encounters by chance.
Shakespeare knew, too. Everything is luck, and not all of it is good.

The Famous Poet's Wife

At the podium, the famous poet is having sex with his wife
in the poem he reads tonight. He uses the four-letter word.

The act is all ankles and elbows, slits and staffs, grunting,
sweating, and unnaturally assumed positions. Naturally,
I'm embarrassed because I can see the famous poet's wife

squirming in her chair as he caresses the heft of her breast,
the eager spread of her knees, and a tiny, beautiful blemish

none of us will ever see. Handy with his tongue, he speaks
of that moment her thighs muffled his ears in her passion

and lingers on a lonely moment when her rush of pleasure
left him behind. The ladies are glassy-eyed. The men nod
and grin. I'm shifting in my seat. The famous poet's wife

slumps as the last line kisses the poet's lips. Some of us clap,
and the applause raises her husband's head from his work.

How I Lost My Library Card

This kid at the library was reading aloud to himself in the corner,
and some old man reading the sports page—wasting time on men
who play with balls for money!—told the kid to shut up, a library,
he said, was supposed to be *quiet,* so *be* quiet, for God's sake,
and of course, in his mind, there was no doubt about who God was.

When I saw the poor kid's surprise, his embarrassment, his shame,
I finally spoke. I said, "Man, *you* shut up. Look, you grumpy fool,
what we have here is a kid reading. He's *reading*! These days,
that's a goddamn miracle. Thirteen hungry, homeless people live
on the library lawn, and you're upset because he's reading *aloud*?

Listen, you dumb bastard, silent reading is for the dead! Are you
hearing me? His lips are moving because those words are alive.
He's speaking aloud because what those words need to revive them
is his breath. He's using his voice because all that story needs
to be heard *is* his voice. So I have an idea. Toss the newspaper

in the trash, and go *play* some damn basketball, instead of sitting
on your flabby ass gazing at numbers about games you never saw.
And while you're at it, find this poor kid a chair, get him a platform,
a podium, a pulpit, put him on a pedestal to shout from his book
in the strongest voice he can raise, and ask him, no, *beg* him, to read

to you, to me, to the library staff, to the patrons, to the thirteen
ravaged souls on the street, and to the rest of this vast, distracted
nation. Let him read his book to us all and make us all one people
for once concerned about what really matters. Let his voice lead us
through a story we need to hear! Let him read! Just let him *read*!"

The Evil Eric
for Eric

Our mutual aversion is a perfect match. On this, we see
                eye to eye. We're hard
to tell apart, for the twain meets in us. Some doubt
                we're twins. We are,

though his eyes of mud mock mine of sky, and my head
                is dark to his light. Ours are
the same scarred, shaven cheeks, baggy pants,
                and flowered shirts. Our lies

are the ones we told as boys. Our postures at the board
                identical, we letter
our lessons in chalk on black in one precise
                and elementary hand. We are equally

dismissed. At the bell, we shoulder the heavy bag of books
                nobody reads but us.
The ones who love us agree with the ones we love,
                and we hate each other

as we must. We are of the same mind. His gladness
                is my misery, yet my misery
makes a misery of his gladness, and I am glad.
                His heart is a dungeon

of pulsing chambers for the black rivers of his blood,
                and truly, in that distinction,
we are definite in our differences, for the blood he drew
                from me was red.

He holds me in high disregard; I duplicate his distaste.
                He loves my work,
but he hates my life, for my success makes his seem small.
                We're a distinctly

differential equation, equal on each side of the sign,
    distributed so differently
we lack the look of balance. Face to face, our profiles
    frame a champion's silver cup,

incomplete without a glare across the gulf, a prize
    neither claims without the other.
Our friends agree on our differences. To familiars,
    we're each a rose known

by the other's name. To all else, we're interchangeable,
    indivisible, with antipathy
and enmity in kind, yet seen together, none thinks us one.
    Duplicates, we are

opposites in opposition. We are two and the same.
    He is the evil one. I am the other.

For the Anniversary of My Death

Every year without knowing, I have passed the day
when my last light will fade, and the earth will turn

away from sunrise, brilliant and blaring, imperious
as any minor moment. My last day will be my first,
a birthday, and though I will not draw breath to kill

      the candles, I know what wishes I will make:

I'll wish for fewer question marks and one last asterisk,
      a tiny typographical star to draw my vision

      to the base of the page, for an apostrophe
to mark my grateful release of shabby possessions
stacked like sentences and old shoes in dimness

beneath wire hangers and a single swinging bulb.
I'll wish to widen the space between lines and letters,

shaping the snowy blankness around me into sense,

and to open landscapes to pines and play and granite.
      I'll wish for an ellipsis trailing into a silver sky
in the thin minute before rain, without the suggestion

of more than there is, with no bow or map to suggest
my passage will leave a path for anyone to follow.

For All You Touch
for Alice Marie Hamilton

Reflected in the glass is a blue harbor edged with white at St. Andrews-by-the-Sea in New Brunswick. In the shop window, on a glass shelf, among Wedgwood china, figures of clay and glass, works of craft and art

and miracles of rare device, is a hand-lettered sign: "You are responsible for all you touch." Within, we find a figure in crystal of a boy

riding a dolphin leaping over waves. Balanced on a transparent tail, the statue trembles at my tread, yet I must stroke the polished clarity of the dolphin's fin and marvel at the solidity of what I can see through.

I drift slowly through bright, narrow aisles. We so often mar or chip or crack or simply break what we touch that we will no longer reach

for china cups and bowls of painted porcelain. We worry that a vase has come so far, from China, from India, from Peru. We dare not touch what is precious and easily lost. Carvings in extinct, expensive grain,

vases fired with forgotten, ancient art, and elegant clocks filigreed with silver, detailed in ivory, inlaid with abalone, and polished, golden

works beneath delicate glass bells are admired and feared. Yet unused, our fine works mean nothing when design is ignored in favor of display. Worth appreciates in knowing teacups chip, saucers crack, and the silver

of the spoon stirring tea tarnishes. Everyday use of our cups and clocks inspires our daily care. As I leave, I affirm we are responsible for all

we touch, for what we reach for, what we grasp and hold and handle, for the grace we find within the whorls of our fingertips, for our works, our small arts, for what we lift, and what we keep, and what we leave.

River Eye

When I stood on the deck above the rivers I loved, felt the wheel turn
in my hands, and stared down at the shifting, murky, muddy curtain
where the Sacramento and the American became one, I was happy

to be where I was. I spent days alone on the deck of the *Damnation*
or drove the *California Kid* against the current into sunset, watching
red-shouldered hawks in cottonwoods overhead. If I did anything

right in those days, it was finding the right things to love and loving
them till they were gone. The world is no better or worse for me
passing through, or for passing through me, bent like the rays sunk

in deep water and glimmers of golden motes in the clouds of silt, soil,
and mud stirred by the flow moving the earth. Everything escapes me
now, so I drop a line into the river, catch what I can, drag snapping,

quicksilver muscle to the deck, and stare for a moment into the cold
and tilting, silver-rimmed darkness of an alien eye from the river bottom
before I release at last what I never meant to catch and cannot keep.

A Silver Flask

Illumination

On those cold, clear winter mornings, I rise in the dark and sit
        beneath a lamp with a pen and paper in a circle of light
barely bright enough for the work. The window beside me is black

and blank, and soon I'm staring only through the window of the page
at whatever I'm drawing from ink and concentration. Hours pass,
        and always, when I least expect it, there's a sudden tide of light

as the sun crests the mountain. When the first rays flood the fields,
the thin, yellow curtain behind me brightens, and the room swells
        with light. Everything is suddenly golden and illuminated,

and for just that one moment, I make the glorious and forgivable
        mistake of thinking it has something to do with me.

Among the Roots

Once, *want* was not desire, but merely
a lack, and not even lack that was need,
but only something missing and noted

in its absence. If a carpenter complained
of a want of lumber, he meant merely
no wood was at hand, and nothing more.

And once, *purpose* meant only daily acts,
as a beaver's purpose is to build his dam
and a rough hutch of sticks, not in service

to some grand design, but because that is
merely what occupies him. *Occupation*
did not yet mean grudging servitude

consuming days in exchange for silver,
but only how hours from dawn to dusk
were spent. And there was even a time,

long ago, when dangerous sea voyages
seeking rich, distant lands yet unplundered
by men from an old and crowded world

was not the only meaning, for *discover*
simply meant seeing what any glance
cast in the right direction would reveal.

McNeil, Arkansas, 1942
for William Stafford

I am glad I was with you in McNeil, when the curious
townsfolk gathered around you, and your friend drawing
a picture, and your friend writing a poem. I was not

in their eyes, narrowed in afternoon light, but I am glad
I was numbered among the pages of Whitman's *Leaves
of Grass* when the suspicious one opened the book

you were reading to seek rhymes in the lines. I was not
in the angry voices rising from throats calling for judgment
upon you, but I was in the delay in fetching the rope

called for in haste. I wasn't in the crowd gladly and grimly
gathering like a storm cloud over the prairie, but I was
in a voice calling from the crowd to summon the sheriff

quick. I wasn't in the order to disperse or the jacketed backs
turned from the ground where you had stood, but I'm glad
I was there in the footfalls and dust rising from the road

back to the sheltering camp. I was not in the late moon
or the stars or the life you began that night, but I'm glad
I was there to save your life so that you could save mine.

City of the Anti-Ghosts

On Thursday, Axel realized everyone
who lived there hated the city.
Not a single citizen loved the parks,

the streets, the drives, the buildings,
the highways, the view. Nobody

loved anything about the place.
They lived there only for their jobs.
Axel knew they hated it because

the sole point of anybody's job
was to service everybody else

who lived in the city, and so on.
If ghosts are souls without bodies,
Axel thought, then his fellow citizens

were anti-ghosts. The city boiled
with bodies void of spirit loitering

in the blue light of televisions
in darkened living rooms.
Axel saw the city was a cipher,

the world a circle of nothing, a zero
scrawled in some divinely obscure

equation. He decided to escape
the endless ends, but when he quit
his job at the mortuary, the newspaper

folded, the bakery collapsed,
the college closed. Main Street

was a wilderness of vacant stores
and traffic lights telling a rosary
of colors in empty intersections.

On Saturday, Axel rented a truck,
loaded furniture and family, and left

his house for sale. His neighbors,
beaten to the punch card, broke
and out of work, fired, laid-off,

"let go," and forced to retire,
watched from sofas on sidewalks.

Beneath frayed brims of caps
from losing teams, they glared
as Axel drove away. His best friend

Zachary lobbed a bottle of light
beer at the grille as Axel passed.

At the city limits, Axel's boss
crouched in the church tower
with a rifle and a clear shot.

Monopoly

Monopoly is a game for winners, not for artless players like me.
I rolled the dice without thought or plan, aiming for exotic places

like Oriental Avenue, which I would fail to purchase. I spent
money and turns and favors to do something elegant like own all
of the red avenues of Kentucky, Indiana, and Illinois, ignoring

the opportunities where I landed. Or I would buy both utilities,
the Electric Company and the Waterworks, instead of keeping

one eye on the market and the other on my cash. Or I bargained
for all four railroads, especially the Short Line, with that wondrous,
intriguing name, instead of purchasing more rewarding property.

Not once did I win. Years later, my brother revealed he'd stolen
hundreds of thousands from the bank. That didn't surprise me
since he was, in those days, a kid. What startled me was the barely

repressed pride, even glee, at his success in thievery and his joy
in the undetected crimes. On that board, I spent an age as short

as a lifetime, circling the same square block on the same streets
with a racing car, a Scottish terrier, and a thimble for companions.
I slowly paid the rising rents to those who had purchased first,

income tax on that square I never missed, even the luxury tax,
always right before I got paid. Later, I watched stunned as cute,
little, green neighborhoods were replaced by ranks of red hotels,

and prices shot up even more, and my cash dwindled to thin bills
of yellow, pink, and white. In the end, I found myself penniless

and amazed, with only one shoe and no direction, in the middle
of some street of strangers, like Pacific Avenue or Marvin Gardens
or Park Place, one roll too far from another payday, sunk and glum

beyond the smirk of prosperity, lost, mystified, and three bills
from broke, counting the last of my cash into my brother's hand.

The Kansas City Grand Emporium Blues

We've drunk in enough bars to know the blues
when the notes begin to bend: after three songs

        at the Grand Emporium, Junior Wells
turns his back on tables crowded with beer
and double shots. The past is drunk and gone.

All we can do is laugh. His parting words
were as sweet as what we almost remember:

        "I got your money, I'm leaving town,
and there ain't nothing you can do about it."

That's the flat-out, broke-down, split-lipped
        humor of the blues. A stunned crowd,
sour in sweat, blue smoke, and the sweet

stink of spilled drinks, watches the bluesman
saunter through a door jamming a slick wad

of cash into his pocket. There's no denying
they paid for what they got. Even crossing

these long miles and dark fathoms changes
        nothing. I like to think, you know,
that even if we stole the cash to engrave

that fine curse in marble, we'd never find
the weedy grave those words might grace.

Should Have Seen It Coming

Stupid as I could possibly be, I slammed down my bleary, half-empty mug
on the ring-marked bar and snarled, "Let's take this outside." I staggered
through jukebox shadows and the stale shades of beer signs to the door.

I stood on the warped green boards of the porch, painted when Jesus
        was learning to ride a bike, and I stopped, swaying and delayed.
Scents of pine and gasoline and garbage and mountain air at altitude

cleared my head, and for a moment, I saw where I was: on a planet
spinning a thousand miles an hour with no help or halt from alcohol,
lit by a sun so far away light takes eight minutes crossing the darkness

to warm me and tickle the trees green. There was a Clark's Nutcracker,
        utterly thoughtless of the name we gave, bopping through branches,
flashy white tail and black-bordered wings on gray in a contrast so sharp

my eyes were utterly and immediately snagged, and my mouth, I'm sure,
considering my condition, fell open. Then, the sun sparked, or I blinked,
or somebody landed one perfectly on my jaw because now, I was staring

straight up, along the thick boles of pines and firs, pointing upward in all
directions blue, rocking a little because the wind was passing through.
Over my head, the nutcracker said, "kraw," as if irony was the order

of the hour, and a bird was here to deliver the news. Oh, man, I laughed.
Strong hands dragged me to my feet, and I threw my arms over shoulders
as we stomped back into the bar roaring, and I bought that man a beer.

A Silver Flask

Of the dead, there is hardly more to say. The man was our appointed poet,
                and our hallowed piles of buttressed stone ring hollow
as we stroll the halls he staggered. Each narrow oaken office door names
                one more lettered, learned man schooled in definitions of "fool,"
"irony," and "comedy," and all taught the gist of our poet, our campus clown,

our dumpy ass in the soiled brown slacks of scuttlebutt. Dead drunks reek,
                yet we indulge their sentimental tales. We linger fondly on stairs
ours bloodied once in a tumble of robes and sashes and stone-cracked skull.
                None can tell how much plaid he peeked beneath or how many shots

he stole from freezers stocked with vodka, though his lines lifted skirts
                and eyebrows less often than his drinking did. He dressed
our spectacles and brought rude, boozy measure to the depth and breadth
                of our successes. We marked his steady wake of brittle books,
smirked at his famed, forgivable contempt for classrooms filled with poets

who read no verse, and ignored the volumes he loved and lent and lost,
                yet we whispered of the crisp winter morning he wept in class
                      at forlorn lines of some scribbler long, long dead. He was
the added dash to our committees and catalogs, to our storied, shaded lanes.

        Beneath pediments scaled with ancient words, he lurched and leaned.
His, the snore through windy speeches we endured. His, the stumbling step,
        the fumble of a treasured tea cup, the vomit in the salad forks,
and rich red carpet swept with elbows, knees, and shirt-tails in a slow,
            sodden crawl beneath the banquet board. Among our ivy and elms,

the man was our monument to the chaos we critique, and his death
                    is prelude to our own proud pageants, yet he was our poet.
        He lived the life we urged him to live. His torments are our footnotes,
his laments, our literature, and our only secret is the gift of a silver flask.

The Priest at Galileo's Deathbed

You've seen enough sunsets to know one
will close tomorrow, too. This day is done,
yet no matter what the gold and purple
                glory, it is not the last.

The time comes for the truth to grace
your departure, even as the stars
                the day hides emerge at dusk.
Look. From this window, light fades,

and night reveals all. I cannot forgive
what you think are your sins. None is
                secret or new. Nothing will cure
or cleanse your deeds. Be still. Tears

change nothing. Absolution is a sweet
myth that well serves those who believe
                their sins great enough
to stun God, the only one who believes

humans worthy in an empty universe
darkening even as we waste our days.
                Death is an empty curse.
Comfort? Take delight in the dying day.

Grip your *Bible* tightly, if you will.
It may as well be a block of the wood
                from which the pages come
for all the good it does in gathering dusk.

No, you are not forsaken. Do you hear
                my words on your last evening?
God has not forgotten us. If he sees,
he never saw our fall. He is beyond us.

Do you remember what you told me?
             The evening star is not a star.
Venus is a planet like ours, but dead.
All are distant rocks reflecting light.

Nor are those stars falling from the sky.
Each is debris burning to reach earth.
                 And the little lights
that seem to our eyes to circle our heads

are merely more distant suns, every one
                   a candle in the window
of a further world where no one dwells.
Hearing your words, I stared at stars

             and saw them anew,
for the suns of the night they are, stars
piercing the blue as the sky darkens.
Those are the eyes of our ancestors,

I once told myself, but they see nothing.
                       Light is blind,
our ancestors are gone, and the stars
you see died long before you were born,

and to what purpose? To travel through
ceaseless darkness without illumination.
Yes, I bless you, but to forgive is to forget.
               You must live in the light

of your regret and follow the dark image
you cast before you on the ground,
          as morning sun sets the shadow
of the plowman before him in the field

he tills, and the dust of which he is made
                 rises from his feet,
as he sows what he hopes may grow
when he passes. His shadow will loom

long at evening, but such is the sun's jest.
No one is so dark or so tall as his shade,
bent and broken on the earth he turned.
                  Fine. Die, if you will,

with your eyes wide. I shall close them.
            Fire from fire, dust to dust.
In the name of the water, the earth,
and the restless wind, none knows

from where we come or where we go,
and even without purpose, the world
         will reach an end, as for you,
the light now dims, even as stars fade

once more in the dawn of another
and another and another day. *Amen.*

Midnight, Snow and Stars

No gods will be born this December eve
                as we stand shod to knees in snow

under hard stars within a black ring of pines
circumscribing sky. At such a moment, we pause
                to ponder the fathomless blue infinite

over our heads and the silence
                ice and the tilt of the planet grant
the land. Starlight illuminates our tracks
        among boles and branches, and the silver
cloud of our breath fades, and gleams, and fades.

Yet when I shake this bough, the weight of winter
                will scatter from limbs and needles
the light of two thousand suns through millions

                or more of miles of darkness.
That darkness encloses me, the same night
         the light crossed with merely an imperative

                  to shine through a blackness
these fierce, fleet rays, falling at my feet
                in glimmering drifts, will never know.
        From a clearing at midnight in a snowy wood,
the universe is too large to bear gods and too small

to bear the light we carry into the darkness we find
        in our eyes when we look toward the stars.

Planets, Houses, and the Night Always Above Us

The celestial houses are ordered and mobile and steady in their progress
        through the night, and I love the dark sky for the perverse illusion
of permanence over the shallow pitch of roofs on Earth, capping only woes.
        Thunder rumbles within, and a pale moon wanes over walls in need
of spackle and paint. I have no counsel, and none would hear me if I did,
so I stand on the grass in a dark yard. All I do is listen and stare at stars.

        In the quiet house behind me, my affections are deep, dull currents
I don't understand any more than I understand the reason for the narrow,
golden zone where life flourishes in a perfect ring and we just happen to be.
My luck is not mine, and the constellations in my heart change only slowly.
The orbits of my hours are regular if elliptical.

        My brain flits around the sun like Mercury,
with days lasting years, and my heart is Jupiter, ponderous, thick, cloudy,
rolling a red eye around, slowly regarding the universe. Orbited by moons
of complexity and wonder, I gaze on glittering rings around a near neighbor,
        marveling without coveting the beauty. I'm a great gas giant
of latitudinal storms and unbreathable elements in winds blowing fast
        and fundamentally through the whorls my thoughts leave on my face.

I'm as bald as Mars, and I cartwheel through my orbit on hands and feet
like Uranus so the sun can kiss my axis, and my other pole directs attention
to darkness. My words are as unexpected and blue and wobbly at the edge
of the universe as Neptune is. My passions are as great as the pressure
on Venus, veiled not for fear but for the wisdom in concealing the heart
        and keeping what we love close.

On the Occasion of Andy's Cancer Diagnosis

On your day in Kula, we'll take a slow, early morning walk
along a narrow, black upcountry road, and we'll head south.

I'll point out the game trails on the roadside. The francolins,
pheasants, and mongoose pass beneath the barbed wire,
        but the deer follow the fence and skirt the last post.

I'll show you the place in the south field where they bed down
in the tall, dry grass. Later, we'll sit in the shade of the porch
and study the groves and gullies of Haleakalā, where the slope
        rises behind the neighbor's house and the papaya grove.

I'll take you to the banana tree where the zebra doves nested
        atop a ripening bunch. We'll pick one blossom each
from the plumeria blooming by the shed. I'll be sure you see

        the first scud of cloud at mid-morning over the mountain.
For lunch, I'll grill hamburgers because we want hamburgers,
potato chips, and soda, for this is summer, and life is short.

We'll sit at the sagging wooden table beneath the kiawe tree
and listen to the cardinal, the finches, and the wind in the grass.

In the hour passing as we eat, we'll watch while the mountain
        disappears beneath swelling clouds. The afternoon
we'll spend reading, reminiscing, and dozing over our poems.

In the evening, we'll see the sun trace a rippling, silver track
        across the sea and follow day to the end. I promise you
the green flash. We'll ponder the high, pink glow over Haleakalā,

which lasts for hours on a perfect evening. As the island darkens,
the sky widens with stars, and I'll show you Venus and Jupiter,
and later, the scorpion and the scales, the balance dim and tipped
        before the claws and coiled tail. After long talk and drink

and midnight, we may hear the deer bawling in the distance,
and we'll take another walk down the road in the dark. We'll see
      a star fall from the night that always encircles us, always,

through all our days, and we'll be grateful for that small, swift light,
though it's fleeting. I will take this walk, and you will be with me.

How to Successfully Flee the Storm

The storm staggers across the roof for five days. Rusty gutters over-
flow and tear from rotten eaves. Rain permeates the creaking house,
your mother's wallpaper rippling and sagging in every room. A stream

quietly descends the stairs. The yellowed ceiling leaks in nine places
in the living room, and the pots plink and plip. Power comes and goes,

and your supper was cold from a can. At last, from the town square,
the courthouse siren winds up to a wail, and the thin sound stops you

on the way from kitchen to bedroom, cup of tea tepid in your hand.
The authorities know best. The time has come to act. You set the cup
on the bookshelf, never to be seen again, not beloved cup, not the tea,

neither shelves nor books nor *Bible*. Your slicker hangs from a hook
in the orange and yellow shape of a cartoon duck. You pause to caress
that childhood decoration, the first time you've touched it in years.

As you turn away, the bedroom vanishes. Behind you in the hall,
the carpet peels away into oblivion, and as you pass, sepia and silver
photos of one hundred and fifty years of your family drop into darkness,

one by one. The names are long gone. The faces follow. Outside,
you hear neighbors curse the sky and the deluge hidden in gray. Still,
there is no thunder, and somehow, that seems wrong. Car doors thunk.

Engines start. Nothing else can be done. You open the front door,
and a chill, wet gust pushes in. The storm owns the place now. You cut

the lights, press the warped door into the frame. Everything in the house
disappears. It's magic. You turn the lock and face the glassy street.

Now, you can weep. Wind snaps and ticks like flames in the trees.
You step to a sodden, leaf-littered walk. The flood has finally come.
You must flee. Everything left to you is ahead. The keys are in your hand.

Hart Crane's Borrowed Raincoat

> "Crane's jump in, of all things, a raincoat, borrowed."
> —Jim Harrison

Crane, desperate on the deck, pelted past ports illuminated
from within, rushing from man to man through the dark,

begging a raincoat from each receding face. His shoes
boomed on the polished boards as he sprinted for the stern

in a steaming rush to the rail, for one last longing look
into eternity while there was still time to contemplate

such a thing. His breath came hard, and the night chilled
his sweaty nape with mist. He looked into the luminescent

wake of the ship, the faint, green track mocking the one
through stars that no longer raised his gaze, as he considered,

perhaps, the short, appalling existence of rain falling from sky
to sea. Eyes dark, he buttoned the borrowed coat, setting

one shoe on the metal rail and pausing at the rumbling thrum
of engines throbbing through his sole, then, in two fierce,

dedicated steps, up, over, and out—a dive into space filled
with the rest of his life. Crane plummeted, with only a raincoat

to shield him from the heaving, freezing sea he leaped
to embrace, watched by the amazed stranger, coatless now,

motionless, a man who had simply worn a raincoat as proper
evening attire for what may fall, unexpectedly, from above.

Man Overboard
after a painting by Christian Krohg

At the hatch, the boy grips bulkhead steel and terror
        in both hands, howling out the terrible news
with the anguish disaster forces from our mouths.
        He is alone on deck, on his first watch,
in the moment of misfortune. But I am not he.

Nor am I the man at the table, so startled in taking
his tea that he pours as the ship rolls, forgetting
        to set the cup beneath the scalding stream,
yet to notice the splashing on the board before him.

        Nor am I the cook, neck arched, head tilted
to peer from the small service window to the galley,
tears already springing to his eyes. And I'm not
the new man interrupted asking after his breakfast,
mind as blank as a student's slate, wiped clean by crisis.

        I am not the cook's mate, shirking dirtier work,
shifting listlessly through a box of oysters for one
easy to pry open, dreaming of a pearl, hearing words
that shock but do not grieve him, already plotting
        to sneak to a quiet berth below and steal a nap.

            Nor am I the bearded man
at breakfast with his newly risen mates, now nodding
after the night's duty, weary and grateful for the bells
that ended his long, dark watch at dawn.

        And I am not the captain, glass in hand,
conning the crew, appointing duties to busy the hands
        with work through a dim, dull day of sailing
for the far fishing grounds to set and haul the nets.

And though I wish I were, I am not the one at ease,
content with pipe packed and gripped in his teeth,
      breathing in the scents of cherry tobacco,
planning a rescue, even as he sets the match to strike.

No, I am the ninth man, the one fallen in the waves,
he whom the boy has deserted to run for the crew.
I am the man he has forgotten to cast the white ring
          hung behind him on the bulkhead
as I choke and spit on the face of crashing fathoms.

     I am he gripped by the freezing green sea,
ice already crusting my hair, cold piercing my flesh,
drinking the heat from my heart and hands beating
at the deep as if this were a fate I might oppose alone.

I am the one unseen, adrift in the fading wake,
kicking boots away and wiping salt from my eyes
           to raise them to a slick, black hull
    and a deck empty of providence. I am lost,

beneath a gray sky in a sea of light and shadow
      with a dark vessel sliding silently past, poised
for the moment the draft or the depths drag me down,
the maws below feast on my limbs, or the line is cast,

      and I am drawn from breaking seas, dripping,
to stand on the deck once more, wrapped in wool
and sipping brandy, among my hapless companions.

An Anatomy of the Celestial

We are not machines of meat, breath, and bone,
no matter what the doctors and determinists say.

Scalpels may sever organs from fresh corpses,
accidental and intentional. Hands gloved in blood
may plop tissue into six-pack-sized beer coolers

to lug life to an operating theater down the hall,
one more miracle that means nothing more
than we treat broken bodies like junked cars.

Yet every last body is all there is of each of us,
one more person constructed of irretrievably

irreplaceable parts. If there is truth in the world,
then where the scalpel slits, the scar marks
the grave of the original. Amended, with plastic

heart or steel-plated joint, you are someone else.
And if you want better light to see this, look again:

our bodies are stars born of night, all drifting,
gathering in darkness gripped by an essential,
eternal gravity, atoms drawn by degrees, each

to each, dust and dark matter in icy emptiness,
molecule by molecule, in a gentle inward spin
into a mass with enough mass to become one

more eruption of light, and light is all we give
the universe. Only that will not diminish us.

The Glad Reaper

Matching Coffee Mugs
for Veronica

At first light, a francolin calls in the field. The cat watches us wake,
speaking the moment our eyes open. Windows pale, and we rise
to start our morning chores. We work together. You feed the cat.

I make the coffee. I set our matching mugs on the kitchen counter,
your name on one, mine on the other. We shower. You carry

spiders in cupped hands to the door and release them in the roses.
I follow you and check the papaya tree. One is ripe. In the dawn,
the skin is golden. You stand by me, and we gaze at the mountain

where the sky glows. The sun soon will reach the ridge. Inside,
I bring bowls and spoons to the table. You tie the curtains back.

A cardinal lights in the kiawe tree. Our eyes open to each other.
I slice fruit on the board, and you toast the bread. I pour coffee
from a brimming pot. You drink from my cup. I drink from yours.

The Woman Who Clears the Way

She sweeps limbs, leaves, and pale fallen blossoms
from our narrow hilltop lane each morning. We hear
the rasp and scrape of stalk on stone, and we make

a game of guessing the tint of the day. Turquoise.
Black. Magenta. Each day, the sweeper dons a dress
of a single shade and, with child dawdling at her feet,

she whisks the night's litter into a pan. Orange. Green.
White. Slowly climbing, broom in hand, back bent,

she clears the way for shoes and hooves and wheels
that will pass through the light. Kneeling near her,
the child pokes a finger at ants among the cobbles,

lifts a pebble or a leaf, or gathers her hem in his fist,
trailing her to the crest of the hill. Saffron. Brown.

Purple. For her, every dawn has a single hue. For us,
valley mist and morning sun unfurl a pale banner
over blue, arcing over black roofs and silver street.

Through the glass, we glimpse the color she wears.
She's chosen red, as perfect and predictable as light
dawn rain, a dress on a new day, or the mango's blush.

Blessings

A deer stood in the road, unmoving in light that seemed brighter
than morning. The velvet horns simply shone. The quiet of forest

and suburban cabins was heightened by the busy hiss of a sprinkler
on a green lawn. Over all, the river spoke only to itself as the water

shoved wet, black boulders and broken branches aside. I looked
for the ouzel I know glides through the spray, but saw only one

robin posed alone on the clipped grass. Stumps in the shadows
gleamed with moss, and bits of their strength littered the driveway

gravel. Sometimes, I wish I could say something significant
about all of this, but I can't. The world speaks louder than I can.

The road to the highway seems longer in sunshine and the river
quieter. And I'm sure if I stop and listen, soon enough, I'll see

a magpie light on the ground, all that glossy black and white
and that mad, fleeting iridescence sunlight strikes from the wings.

The Awk Word

The awk word just sticks out, jabs the reader in the eye,
and never in a good way. The awk word leaves all

to be desired, all stones unturned, well enough undone.
The awk word drops like a shard between a hard place
and a harder place. When one chooses the awk word,

there are no fireworks, no boom, no boon, no boost,
not the gleam, gloom, glamour, or glimmer of the light

that ought to shine through ink; instead, a smudge marks
the wrong turn of a drafthand stumbling from boulevard
to bramble. The awk word forces the reader's pen

        to the verge to scrawl what should emerge only
in a squawk from the craw of a crow or a raving raven.

A clipped cry in a wilderness of rock, riven by ragged
scrub and brush, the awk word descends from on high
like any of many odds plunging dumbly to crush a skull,

which, deserving or not, will still split, crack, or burst
beneath the burden of the inept, unbalanced, and graceless.

Eating Crow

A forkful of feathers and broken wings is hard to swallow, but I will.
I won't say I'm sorry. Let's be cold and clear on that. I'm not sorry,

even if I was wrong. Just serve the unpardonable pie. Score with iron
tines a crust fledged in black. Chop the meat to mince from the worst

bits of bird—talons, toes, gizzard, neck, skin, hollow bones, and gravel
from the guts, jerked and dried in the dark. Bake a thick crust black,

and sprinkle on some sugar. Such may trick my lips, may make tasty
a foul dessert, may turn the sour savor sweeter. Bring the pie piping,

straight from the stove, and fetch my twisted wooden spoon. If I cram
the dish down, I will scorch my stupid tongue and never taste a morsel.

The Word-Swallower

There is no charge for admission to the green, mildewed tent
staked slackly in an alley of the midway between a cotton candy
cart and ping-pong toss. Billed an attraction, the word-swallower

is not. Few come to observe him, seated on a steel, folding chair,
beneath a single spot in a vacant, shadowed, curtained room,
enshrined in silence. He swallows words. His silence is golden.

No matter how keen the verbiage rising to his tongue, no matter
        how many edges on each unspoken word that comes to mind,

his tent is hushed but for the whispers of visitors who mark well
his silent line of lips. He answers no questions, retorts to no quip,
responds to no riposte, and his attendant dog-faced boy at the door

tells every dusty bumpkin a grim, dismal tale. Says the boy,
        "If there were a king of the carnival, a lord of the boardwalk,

the word-swallower is not he. He hasn't spoken since he learned
        to talk. With no words for his wisdom, he speaks none.
Philosophers divide our sullen species from the other chimpanzees

        by the power of speech, but the word-swallower knows finer
and says naught on this or any other subject." The word-swallower

denies nothing. He fears no loss in lack of speech. He keeps peace
battened like a castle under siege and guards an armory of lustrous
weapons best left beyond reach. From imaginary battlements, each

word slips behind the tongue, lies sunk in the gullet, plummets
        to the gut. Lips sealed, tongue unbitten, his thought hardens

beneath the red fist beating the bars of his chest and the bellows
burning breath into a world soundless and pointless without words.
        At dusk, the word-swallower and dog-faced boy stroll

into the hills of a trim town noisy with streetlit night. The boy barks.
The word-swallower strokes the curly fur on the boy's ears, creeping through charged darkness and the grandiloquence of stars.

The Lessons of Moonlight

Since we must celebrate death, let us
                         leave it to the children.

We'll cradle bowls of coins and candy,
                 awaiting a knock at the door,

while they learn the lessons of moonlight
           from fallen leaves and caramel apples—

         to enter a darkening world
                   dressed as monsters,

         to read fate in sidewalk cracks
               through holes in plastic masks,

         to seek treats with pretty threats
              at the doors of strangers.

The Glad Reaper

    In fields great and green as new grain, Death grins
as he swings his scythe, and why shouldn't he be happy?
    He has the best job in the world. He's got benefits.
He's productive and appreciated. He frees the suffering.
    He awards the meek their inheritance, and he drives
the proud to ground. His fences are true, long and strong,
    and there's always enough rain. He's the local agent
for Evolution County. He knows all about crop rotation
    and curving his furrows to fit the slope of the soil.
Darwin is his guide, God's on his side, and he cannot lose.

    The sun shines on his daily labors. The wide sky
is relentlessly cheerful blue. The few clouds are chubby
    seraphs that give the infinite a glad character
and bring occasional shade to his work. Death wears
    the classic overalls, always new blue nearly black,
loose and stiff, with plenty of pockets, buttons, and loops
    for tools. He has a hobby: he collects last words,
though few are worth hearing. The last words of most
    are a fervent curse or a bleat of surprise, but Death
has a fine sense of humor. He gleefully seeks the ironic.

    With a smile, he recalls Goethe croaking, "More light!
More light!" Death is immortally happy. He will outlive us
    all. He sweeps a scythe that will never ever sever
his own slender neck. He's nearsighted. He carries with him
    spectacles he rarely wears, and he never sees
a face till he's a heartbeat away. This evening, comfortable
    in the farmhouse parlor he still calls a drawing room,
he'll don those glasses. He'll pour himself a whiskey neat,
    settle in a doilied armchair, pleasantly over-stuffed,
and chuckle in a cozy circle of lamplight over poems taunting
    his pride and his strength, his fierce and lazy grace.

The Whistle

Nobody on our tufty, scrubby diamond sees darkness does not fall.
Dusk creeps from grass, climbs trees, and rises from beneath our feet

to dim the sky. None of us, crouched here on the field, sees the earth
        is the source of darkness. Around the lot, shadows knot
themselves together. Soon, they cover the street, sidewalk, grass,

        and field. I can't see the batter or pitcher, so I gaze at the sky
as stars populate that far, purple zone of myth. I cover the outfield,

right, left, and center. The baseball appears as a sudden white sphere
        long after the crack of the bat. I sweep the fly from the night
as much to save my skull as to end the inning. The seven of us go

through the motions because no one wants to say the game's over.
Nobody wants to call this one even though we all want to go home.

Play goes on, and the light fails and dims our vision. Then, we hear
        my father's whistle, piercing and unmistakable, the three notes
that command our presence. We bolt toward the infield. I swoop past

the trash-can lid near the batter's box, grab our bat and extra glove,
tear toward the street and up the hill. The fervent slapping of our soles

on sidewalks echoes from red bricks and yellow windows as we pass,
and the sound is a scatter of brats, racing through twilight to rooms
        of light. I turn toward home—no outs, no ups, no thought—

rounding the corner to my door, and arriving, before that red-veined,
white orb descends from designs stitched in darkness over my head.

The Godzilla Delusion

for Melanie, whose compassion is boundless

Like so many of us, Godzilla believes he's bigger than he is.
      He takes up so much space because he thinks he needs it,
yet Godzilla fears he's smaller than he is, and as we do, he moves

          with grand gestures and great leaps that devastate
and obliterate. He treads the beds of roses he has come to enjoy.

      The resemblance is clear when Godzilla believes he's cuter
than he is, convinced of his own good looks, green, nubbly, ugly
      monster that he is. Like ours, his own face is familiar

and fine with him when he gazes into the mirrored surface of a lake.
      As we do not, Godzilla doesn't know how bad his breath is.

None of us realize either that a mere clearing of the throat delivers
          a torch of fire that scorches land and man and beast
and machine. Godzilla reminds me of me when he believes

      he is being clear. His roars are whispers to his ears,
and he repeats himself, announcing, "Hey, it's only me. It's me,

guys. Hello? Here I come." Like so many of us, Godzilla glows
      with self-regard, radioactive, deadly, and dreaded
by the fleeing multitudes. I know I don't, and Godzilla doesn't

know his own strength. How could he? We're all one of a kind.
      Like us, he has nothing for compare but skyscrapers

and aircraft carriers, mountains and molehills. Like you and me,
      Godzilla never stops to appreciate the little things in life.

He can't see them, and his clawed paws crush cars and tanks
      and trucks and entire nuclear families as he keeps his eye
on bigger things. As we do, Godzilla always wanted to visit Japan,

for the sushi, kabuki, and saké, a little Tokyo night life,
a visit to the cherry blossom festival, and just as we would not,

       he did not recognize Ueno Park when he left
a wake of smashed branches, busted benches, and a breezy scatter

of pale petals. Like me and you, Godzilla has no sense of history,
       or decorum, or proportion, or humor, and most important,
no sense of responsibility, and as our spitting image, Godzilla

       leaves the wrack and ruin of his passage for survivors
to repair. As any of us do, Godzilla remembers his childhood

as magic, gazing sunward through a rosebush, whose leaves
       are black in the brilliance and whose blooms scent
the air with inescapable, eternal fragrance. Godzilla believes,

       deep down, in a way each of us finds endearing
about ourselves, that in spite of what the loudspeakers command

       or where the bullets fly or missiles fall, truly deep down,
everybody loves him, and all want the best for him. Like any of us,
       Godzilla is an innocent beast, who deserves all

he'll be denied, a sunny, sandy beach, a jasmine scent of heaven,
       a warm blue sea, and all the fish he can eat. I see myself,

and all of us, in Godzilla, believing this world is finer than it looks
       and the next horizon encompasses the last heaven on earth
if only we can crush these tiny, pesky armies that oppose us.

My Brother's Keeper

I know you love me. I am always able to take from him
whatever I will. When Cain sought your hand, I vowed
to take you even as he brought you silks and slippers.

When he saved his gold, I stole all and squandered it
on dice and wine and whores. What he cannot keep
belongs to me. Are you not weeping proof of that?

When we were boys, behind my father's back, I struck
my brother, and when my father turned, he saw Cain
spring on me unprovoked and in a rage. He is mine.

Everything he has is mine, even his memories belong
to me. Behold. When he was young, he rode the goat
to market with my father, but I stole the story for my own,

and now, when my father tells the tale, he recalls me
as the son neighbors cheered and laughed to see
ride a goat into the village. As I will with you, I do

with him what I will. I have made my mark on him,
as I mark all that I own, as I have marked even you
with a sign he will know. Cease your cursed weeping!

The wound will heal, and you will find another man
to mount. The fool may even forgive you. He is weak,
and I shall take his place as my father's first son,

for my offerings show God's favor, and in God's eyes,
I am the first son. There shall be no sons before me.
On your feet, woman! In God's holy name, be dressed

and begone! Yes, tell my brother all you wish to tell.
Cain is a small man with eyes only for earth. The sky,
he watches only for falling rain. He believes the earth

the source of life. He would surely settle in one house
to live all his days. He would squat on the land to root
like a pig or an olive tree, never to know the wonders

of wandering the world. There's no future in tilling earth.
One takes, and moves on. Our God lives in the sky.
Cain's lack of faith offends me, so I foul his offerings.

When he plows, I drive my flock through his fields.
The earth is dirt and gives only grain, but I slay sheep
for meat, for blood shows strength in the swift hand

that slaughters. Spare him? Never. Here is my moment,
my triumph, my victory. At noon, I will find him digging
in the dirt. I will tell him you are faithless, yes, tell him

you have lain with his beloved brother, and we will test
his love. Yes, I know he will forgive you. He loves you.
Cain's heart holds no mysteries, nor does the future.

My hope is you will bear him my son. Let God's will
be done! I will save that fine jest for last. Today, he tills
fields to the east, and there, I will have all that is mine.

The Eye of Winter

        Walking the woods, we tread bright frozen ground.
What once was a pond, freezing inward from edges,
            has become an irised eye of ice, staring through trees

into a silver sky. The lidless eye of winter glares from the forest
        floor, and that cold gaze regards dubious clouds.

                Beneath our boots, snow creaks, but ice is silent,
oak leaves beneath and one frozen within. Only one eye
        opens where water pools within a crease of leafless trunks

rising from frozen earth. Nearly naked limbs allow light to fall
        on the places darker in summer, and now, the eye of winter
stares into an amplitude of stars, glimmers as we reflect on ice

        from a day of wandering steps in a place the path is lost.
Limbs bow, and twigs topple into this unblinking frozen eye
        peering into the universe. Silence is the sound of winter,

            and there is no color in these circles and no vision
in the eye of winter, even with everything to see in the direction

we rarely look, up to the light, up to the bending of rays
        into colors that blind us, up to the ringing sky
            shielding us from all we are meant to see.

Our Little Piece of Sky

We drove our little piece of sky home and parked it in front
of the house. Blue as the day is long, that little piece of sky
shone at the curb beyond the brilliant emerald of the berm.

If a road is a river, our little piece of sky was a raft launched
for travel on a massive, mud-muscled surge between clouds
and the current. Wind rocked our little piece of sky, and rain

illuminated the curves. Our little piece of sky burned beneath
the sun, silvered in the moon, and sparked among the stars.

If there were a valley and a bay to reflect on, our little piece
of sky was a mirror and a mind made to reverse the vista.
If there were a forest, our little piece of sky hummed among

the crowns and limbs and leaves. If there were mountains,
our little piece of sky edified pinnacles and peaks. Aimless

aboard our little piece of sky, we allowed the flow to bear
us resolute in the direction we knew the future lay, no regrets
at a constant southerly compass, no reverence for the great

wheels on vessels toiling upriver toward the inexplicable,
and no fear for the imminent delta, or for the sudden gulf,
or for the broken, breaking sea that overcomes all that comes.

Luminaria on Wellesley Drive: Albuquerque, 1978
for Judith L. Florence

When the luminaria were lit, the eve began, the dark part
      at least, beneath stars and stubborn illumination

from the night. Luna was in the sky, a bright face glum
with reflections of the luminous eclipsed by the turning
of the world. On the sidewalk were brown paper sacks

bottomed with river sand from the south valley, burning
      candles within casting a glow of gold on snow,
while the light of the stars looks electric, cold and chaotic.

      Every last breath drifts into blue, deep and sparked
with old light. If the night were mine, I'd carry the title
to darkness with my hands in my pockets, but my fists

are knotted on nothing, and the sky lifts my eyes to look
      through the clouds from my mouth and see the cold,
universal turning that will end the eve, the winter, the world.

All I know is love dies as every voice and vision passes,
and days grow lighter or darker as seasons come and go,
and since I know that, I know all will end, even eventually

me. The street is empty with moon and candles and snow
and stars, and with all that light, there's nothing I can't see.

A Million-Dollar Bill

on hearing of the incident in North Carolina

Nobody at Wal-Mart knows anything about the really high
denominations of bills. After all, those red-jacketed losers
work for minimum wage, and they probably never even saw
a hundred-dollar bill. I have. They're real pretty, especially
those new big-head Franklins. A million is a magic kid-dream,

like "I wish I had a million dollars." There must be a bill for that
beautiful number, so I made one for me. The one thing I can do
is draw, so I got some green ink-pens, measured a piece of paper
with a dollar, and went to work. I copied numbers and signatures
from the one I had and added all the warnings, seals, and capital

Latin quotes. I traced lines and designs, every word: "This Note
is Legal Tender for All Debts, Public and Private." That sounds
official. I even used Bill Gates in the portrait. Who else, right?
The face and backside took me a month of Saturdays to finish,
but when you're making something valuable, you take your time.

Plus, you know, the wife and kids were driving me crazy, five kids
dragging me to soccer games and malls and drive-thru windows
all the time. And I always need to keep a little peace with the wife
or at least hold life down to a dull roar. Now, folks will be joking
about that. One reporter said a million is like me and my family,

one trailed by a bunch of zeroes. Funny. At the store, I needed
to spend enough to make the bill convincing, so I loaded the cart
with a microwave oven, thirty or forty rolls of toilet paper, some
toothpaste, dog food, a gross of Pampers, and some new DVDs,
Ocean's Eleven, *The Great Train Robbery,* and *The Italian Job.*

The wife's been wailing for years for a new vacuum cleaner,
so I picked up one of those, too. When I got to the check-out,
I handed over that beautiful bill, green with patience and promise,
and while the cashier held my work up to the light, I stood there
in line, grinning, thinking about all the change coming my way.

Notes

Cleaning Up After the Storm is an epithalamion for Joella and Steve Arment, who were married on August 23, 2014.

A Festival of Crescents: During a solar eclipse, the image of the sun is refracted through any narrow opening between the light and the ground, where the varying shapes of sun appear as the eclipse progresses. My friend Andrew Ehrmann pointed out these images, seen on the sidewalk by the hundreds through the wind-tossed limbs of a tree, and stopped me in my tracks.

For the Anniversary of My Death: This is a homage that begins by adopting and adapting the first line of W.S. Merwin's famed poem of the same title.

Hart Crane's Borrowed Raincoat: This fine line is from Jim Harrison's poem "North American Image Cycle." Hart Crane, author of the classic American poem sequence *The Bridge,* committed suicide by leaping overboard from the deck of the steamer *Orizaba* on April 27, 1932.

Man Overboard: This poem is based on the painting *Man Over Bord* by Norwegian painter Christian Krohg, which was completed in 1905 and, confusingly, shares the same title with a number of the artist's other canvases, perhaps originally a series. The painting to which I refer depicts seven men at table in a ship's galley at the moment another crew member announces the news.

The Word-Swallower: I'm a great lover of carnivals, and my eye gravitates to stories about them. Once, as I read a list of performers, I misread "the sword-swallower."

A Million-Dollar Bill: In December, 2011, a man was arrested for allegedly attempting to purchase goods at a Lexington, North Carolina, Wal-Mart using a million-dollar bill of his own design.

Acknowledgments

Grateful acknowledgment is made to the editors of the following publications, in which these poems are forthcoming, first published, or reprinted.

Bamboo Ridge: Illumination

Chiron Review: Fortuitous; The Priest at Galileo's Deathbed

Cider Press Review: A Festival of Crescents; Matching Coffee Mugs; Midnight, Snow and Stars

Clerestory: Poems of the Mountain West: Blessings; Cleaning Up After the Storm; McNeil, Arkansas, 1942

COLLECT: Man Overboard

Confrontation: Our Little Piece of Sky

Crossing Lines (A Main Street Rag anthology): Exploring the House Next Door When Nobody's Home; How I Lost My Library Card

Event (Canada): An Anatomy of the Celestial

The Fiddlehead (Canada): On the Occasion of Andy's Cancer Diagnosis

Gargoyle: The Godzilla Delusion

Going Down Swinging (Australia): A Million-Dollar Bill; Monopoly

Hampden-Sydney Poetry Review: Among the Roots

Hawai'i Pacific Review: The Lessons of Moonlight; The Whistle

Hawai'i Review: For the Anniversary of My Death

Heavy Bear: Watermelon Seeds

Iota (England): A Silver Flask

James M. Vaughan Award for Poetry (2009): The Whistle

The Los Angeles Review: My Brother's Keeper

Lummox: Should Have Seen It Coming

Magma (England): The Woman Who Clears the Way

MARGIE: Eating Crow

The New Zoo Poetry Review: An Alchemy of Soap and Seeds and Cinders

The Next Review (England): The Evil Eric

North American Review: The Famous Poet's Wife; Hart Crane's Borrowed Raincoat; How I Lost My Library Card

Oregon Literary Review: Watermelon Seeds; The Woman I Might Have Been

Poetry NZ (New Zealand): River Eye

The Quadrant Magazine (Australia): The Awk Word

Quantum Leap (Scotland): Exploring the House Next Door When Nobody's Home

RATTLE: The Word-Swallower

San Pedro River Review: Luminaria on Wellesley Drive: Albuquerque, 1978

Slant: The Kansas City Grand Emporium Blues

Southword Journal (Ireland): A Telephone

Spillway: The Glad Reaper

The Stand Magazine (England): City of the Anti-Ghosts; The Eye of Winter; For All You Touch; How to Successfully Flee the Storm

Stone Voices: Among the Roots

The Sugar House Review: The Printer

The Sun Magazine: Illumination

Turtle Island Quarterly: Planets, Houses, and the Night Always Above Us

About the Author

Eric Paul Shaffer is author of eight books of poetry, including *Lāhaina Noon*; *Portable Planet*; and *Living at the Monastery, Working in the Kitchen*. More than 600 of his poems have been published in the USA, Australia, Canada, England, Ireland, Japan, New Zealand, Scotland, and Wales. Shaffer received Hawai'i's 2002 Elliot Cades Award for Literature, a 2006 Ka Palapala Po'okela Book Award for *Lāhaina Noon*, and the 2009 James M. Vaughan Award for Poetry. He won a fellowship to attend the Summer 2006 Fishtrap Writers Workshop and was a visiting poetry faculty member at the 23rd Annual Jackson Hole Writers Conference in 2015. Shaffer teaches composition, literature, and creative writing at Honolulu Community College.

www.ingramcontent.com/pod-product-compliance
Lightning Source LLC
Chambersburg PA
CBHW052122070526
44586CB00016B/2043